GLOBE

The Wesleyan Poetry Program:
Volume 101

GLOBE

ELIZABETH SPIRES

WESLEYAN UNIVERSITY PRESS
MIDDLETOWN,
CONNECTICUT

ACKNOWLEDGMENTS

Some of the poems in this book originally appeared in the following magazines:

American Poetry Review: "Courtesan with Fan" (originally titled "Geisha"); *Antaeus:* "Snowfall," "Dark Night on Cape Cod," "Sun in an Empty Room"; *Bulletin of the Poetry Society of America:* "Letters to the Sea"; *Carleton Miscellany:* "Salem, Massachusetts: 1692"; *College English:* "Flashback"; *The Georgia Review:* "The Travellers"; *Hudson River Anthology:* "Exhumation"; *MSS:* "Skins"; *The New Yorker:* "Tequila," "Widow's Walk"; *The Paris Review:* "After Three Japanese Drawings"; *The Partisan Review:* "Instructions for the Sleeper," "The Telescope"; *Ploughshares:* "Blue Nude," "Blame"; *Poetry:* "Globe," "Boardwalk," "Catchpenny Road," "Death Dress"; *The Yale Review:* "Wake"

Some of these poems also appeared in the chapbook *Boardwalk*, published by Bits Press (special thanks to Bob Wallace).

The author would also like to thank William Gifford, Vassar College for the W.K. Rose Fellowship in the Creative Arts, the Ohio Arts Council for an Individual Artist's Grant, and the Corporations of Yaddo and MacDowell Colony for residencies.

Library of Congress Cataloging in Publication Data
Spires, Elizabeth.
    Globe.
    (Wesleyan poetry program ; v. 101)
    I. Title. II. Series.
PS3569.P554G57   811'.54   81–725
ISBN 0–8195–2101–9   AACR2
ISBN 0–8195–1101–3 (pbk.)

Distributed for Wesleyan University Press by Columbia University Press, 136 South Broadway, Irvington, N.Y. 10533

Manufactured in the United States of America   First edition

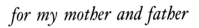

for my mother and father

CONTENTS

III

TEQUILA

I live in a stone house high in the mountains,
close to the stars . . .
                          Last night, a little lonely,
I went to the bar in the valley
where the regulars tell their stories,
one about a man with a runaway dog,
who stood by his door each night calling
Tequila, Tequila. Nobody
knew how long his grief would last
or what he did when his house went dark.
Did he sit all night tipping
a bottle of tequila to his mouth,
legs wrapping the bottle in warmth
the way a shot of tequila
wraps the throat? Or did he sleep
like everyone else, holding his parts
close to himself like a dog? Nobody should
go near a man who wants to be
that lonely. Nobody does.
Bragging, I told them I'd go back
to any year in my life
and live it over. I lied
and said nothing had ever scared me.
They looked at me, all husbands and fathers.
The stars will blind you, they warned,
the ghosts in the alley
will blow smoke in your eyes and steal
your money. I nodded, pretending to know.
But someday I'll leave this place with
only as much as I can carry,
taking the only road
out of the valley, the one that leads

everywhere. And though I'm not friendly,
I'll leave a note on the door,
black writing on a white square, cryptic
and small, so the regulars can make up
my story: *Gone to find Tequila* —

I

GLOBE

I spread my game on the cracked linoleum floor:
I had to play inside all day.
The woman who kept me said so.
She was middle-aged, drank tea in the middle of the day,
her face the color of dust layered on a table.

A high window let in alley light
to a two-room apartment.
Sofas and chairs bristled like hedgehogs
and made the back of my legs itch.
No red flowers on the windowsill. No radio.
Just waxy vines drooping over the tables,
a dome clock dividing time into fifteen-minute parcels.

What did I do all day?
Made card houses so frail
I had to turn my breath the other way.
Or colored the newspaper comic strips,
or wobbled across the floor in my mother's old pumps
with the aplomb of somebody drunk.

Enter my father at 5:15, dark and immediate,
finished with his shift at the factory.
He was hiding something behind his back.
He turned as I circled him,
keeping whatever it was out of sight.
Close your eyes and hold out your hand —
I touched a globe slotted on top for coins,
my hand shadowing the continents
like a cloud thousands of miles wide.
He put my finger over the state where we lived,
then handed me his loose change to fill the world with.

Memory's false as anything, spliced in the wrong parts,
queerly jumping. But better than forgetting.
We walked out into the soft light of October, leaves
sticking to our shoes like gold paper.
I was four years old and he was twenty-five,
same age as I am writing this.

THE TREE-OF-HEAVEN TREE

I remembered the stars, but not the moon.
It was a different moon, but different
in what way? I remembered the shadows
of trees more clearly than the trees,
the sound of rain but not the sound of
my mother's voice.

Jean Rhys

It's time to go to sleep.
I'll put out the light.
— And so the nights of my childhood,
a thousand of them, two thousand,
collect themselves,
are counted as one night,
as all stories are one story
told to the child
once, twice, three times,
by the mother bent over the child's bed,
framed in the doorway's outer radiance,
her face all darkness.
Once, twice, three times,
and still asked for again
on the fourth night!
Until the story tells itself,
ending where it began,
or shedding its skin,
the story within the story
slipping out,
as the soul in sleep
slips in and out of the body,
travelling only half as far as it might,
always returning before morning.

*

Sick all winter, feverish,
I lay in the dark, my narrow bed
rocking a little like a rowboat,
pointing me north like a compass.
I lay in the dark
waiting for that zero minute
when the house would run down,
and everything would have to stop,
even the night
hanging stiffly outside the window.
Only the moon
could slip sidewise
across the sky, trailing
a silver line that snagged
on stars and houses,
my bed sliding toward the window,
tugged by the moon's white hand —
until I fell, end over end,
down a dark tunnel
into the arms of my mother.
Was it a dream?
Had she waited all night to be there?
I woke up not knowing
where I had been,
or where I was now,
the dark room turned a little,
my bed still anchored to the wall.

*

January. February. March.
Counting the months to myself,
I watched a dark hand
tear the calendar's pages off,
each month as long
as the hours in a night.
I watched my mother's body swell,
the skin across her stomach
pulled tight
as the skin of a white apple.
She had swallowed a seed
that grew and grew,
making a tree inside her.
Soon she would leave for awhile,
the white owl taking its place
in the tree of heaven
to cry to the stars and moon —
a signal for me to slip out
the window and run away.
My parents would call and call,
but no one would ever find me.

*

Up in the tree of heaven,
the moon was enormous.
Caught on the highest branches,
it was bleeding silver light.
The moon-faced owl sat in shadow —
close enough to touch —
if I looked at it sidewise,
its face looked a hundred years old.
It never said a word
but let me stroke its feathers,
the night air was like ether
and I slept and slept.
I knew that summer was over
when we both began to shiver,
the owl unfolded its wings
pulling me closer.
Down and down and down,
we flew in a dizzy spiral,
fast as a falling star, maybe
faster. Black wind rushing,
I fell into my bed,
the owl flew to my mother
and hung above her head.
Its feathers fell off like snow —
it wasn't an owl at all!
My mother sang a song
and held it in her arms,
but it kept on crying and crying,
like a baby that's just been born.

*

Outside the moon was still moving,
falling toward the future
but never getting there.
The bare black arms of trees
twisted upward
to nowhere. It was winter again!
My brother slept in a bed,
with bars to keep him in—
if I reached across the dark,
I could almost touch him.
Where are your feathers, little owl?
What did you do with them? —
I sang the words in my head.
But he slept on and on,
forgetting the tree of heaven.

SKINS

Above my head the apples on my grandparents' tree
glowed with a pale green light.
I swung on the swing
waiting for them to drop.
Then walked on them, a balancing act,
with unsteady five-year-old feet.
Skins split.
Something sweet floated out and caught to my feet
following me everywhere — past grape arbor
and chicken coop, a trellis of roses and onion patch,
down to an unused outhouse bordering an alley of dust.

I forget what the world meant to me then . . .
people and objects swam past, not bothering
to explain themselves or tell me where they were going.
Like the goldfish cruising in my grandparents' fishpond
mouths frozen over O-shaped syllables of air
that rose to the surface and popped.
The largest was the size of my hand, its papery skin
an orange bruise that swelled and swelled
as I threw it too much bread.
Was it true a fish would explode if it ate too much?
It was something I'd heard and wanted to see proof of.
The big fish was puffing into a balloon
the week my parents came to take me home.

An early frost froze all the fish into glass floats.
I sat in first grade awkwardly
cutting a fish out of construction paper for a reading race.
My blunt-edged scissors got the tail too long,
the snout pointed and menacing like a shark's.
I printed my name in block letters on the spine, watched
the teacher skewer it with pins to the bulletin board.
What was it like to be stuck in the wrong element
waiting for a thaw? Everything beyond yourself
out of control and no way to move backward or forward?
Dead. The word meant having your eyes sewed shut
and ice water for blood. Above my head a column of fish
swam in blue cellophane, aiming toward a finish line
of yarn. Each day my fish would edge forward,
beating out the others, gold stars stuck to its fin.

FLASHBACK

All afternoon the light falls
on our bodies like thin, invisible nets. It's July;
albino fathers, filled with unrest,
run up and down the beach awkwardly tossing beach balls
against the wind. The ocean pushes against the sky,
flattens it into a blue plate hovering above
our heads. Arms interlaced, we lie
in the sand, young and "almost in love,"
languid somnambulists on the verge of waking.
I rouse myself, put my ear to your chest,
and hear waves breaking —

At ten I spent my summers in Ohio
reading mermaid stories and musty books about the sea.
I imagined the green sharks' teeth of the tide,
    beaches littered
with stranded whales, anemones
sprouting vegetable-like. Sunday afternoons,
    in Great Aunt Sophie's
parlor, I sat on the horsehair sofa
admiring her cabinet of curios.
The best was a giant nautilus, the trophy
of a vagabond, I thought, not a spinster who
    collected china
shoes and music boxes. *A birthday present*
when I was twenty . . . was all she'd say,
never referring by name to her long-dead fiancé.
Its inner sea chambers glittered,
secret as a snail, faintly phosphorescent —

I'm twenty. This is Delaware. You've brought
me here unaware of reveries
I harbored as a child. Awake, not
dreaming, I'm afraid of sand crabs and dead fish,
rainbows rotting on their fins. And of the ocean at night.
It's late afternoon; the last few swimmers
run up the beach wearing their towels like capes.
You kiss the nape
of my neck, then pull me down to the tideline.
On the horizon, night shimmers
like a mirage of inky squid. A little girl again,
I sight
the first star, Venus, rising slowly in the west,
and start to make a wish. You carry me into the ocean,
holding me tightly against your chest.

BOARDWALK
for David

Tonight
these messages
we pencil into picture postcards
to send to friends
who live inland, who never visit the ocean,
seem scrawls of omission: *dolphins sighted*
and lost . . . fishermen on the jetty in yellow raincoats . . .
the boardwalk's arcade of lights . . .
We sleep in a rented house
that offers no protection against nightmare:
the black wave high as a house
rising against us, or fog
walling us in
until, like sleepwalkers,
we break the windows with our hands
and let the night rush in to fill each room's emptiness.

An arcade of lights . . .

We can go to the shooting gallery,
a Wild West Saloon, and aim for the piano player
frozen over an upright
riddled with bullet holes. Hit the spittoon,
and his head spins round,
his left foot taps out time
to a fragment of honky-tonk played over and over.
We can ask Sister Lisa to advise, impersonating
lives we've studied on the boardwalk,
gestures of boredom and desire.
She'll open our hands like old maps,
look into our palms and lie, pretending
we'll have many children.

We can have our picture taken by a photographer
with a trunkful of costumes. He'll pose us,
stone-sober, in front of painted backdrops
from plays and novels: a cherry orchard,
a train station, a *fin de siècle* drawing room.
His old-fashioned flash
blinding us, so that we stagger
back onto the boardwalk holding each other,
unsure which way to go.
On either side of us, more mirrors
and lights, more hours to kill
until the boardwalk closes at one or two.

Tomorrow
we'll sleep till noon. Or maybe
I'll wake early and quietly leave you
to walk the empty boardwalk, arms around myself,
reassured by the clarity of morning,
gulls scavenging, the smell of coffee
coming from the coffeeshop.
I'll mail the stack of postcards
left on the nightstand, dating them
Yesterday, Today, or *Tomorrow,*
pencil two stick figures into your favorite view —
a curving panorama of the ocean —
who wave and wave,
their backs to a breaking wave
held
in the split second before it crashes around them,
the dull grey sheen of the sun
(unseen but felt) slanting even as it does now

on a jigsaw of boards and swollen pilings,
shops and tents and rides
closed tight, roped down,
covered over like expensive merchandise,
the ocean glittering as if
someone had been polishing it all night.

CATCHPENNY ROAD

Summer ends tonight.
Air cuts into our lungs
as frost cuts the field
into flowers. Stars catch
in the pond's dark water
drawing us farther
from the lighted houses.
We catch our arms
in circles round our chests
as if this were protection
against darkness.

Spiked firs border the road.
Behind each one are ghosts
whose names we don't know,
who watch us, who
withhold themselves,
who'd never hurt us.
They come to you in your sleep,
sit in a circle round your bed,
saying the things the living
want to say and can't.
You try to move your head, try
to move into their world of light
where the lace on the child's
white dress burns your skin
like a kiss. But no,
touching their lips to yours,
they go, wordlessly and without cause,
as only the dead might.

Mist spills from the trees
as you talk and we walk
from valley to hill, hill to valley,
till we come to the place
where we left off, unmarked road
crossing itself in the dark.
Blackened by frost, leaves
blow over the pond,
absorbing the water's stain,
sinking toward the stars' reflections.
You kneel, smooth the water
with your hands, and say nothing.
The dead surround us, holding
stones in their hands like coins.
Money they would lend us.

II

WIDOW'S WALK

When he visited Nantucket, Crevecoeur noted,
"A singular custom prevails here among the
women. . . . They have adopted these many years
the Asiatic custom of taking a dose of opium
every morning; and so deeply rooted is it,
that they would be at a loss how to live
without this indulgence".

Walter Teller,
Cape Cod and the
Offshore Islands

Captain: the weathervane's rusted.
Iron-red, its coxcomb leans into the easterly wind
as I do every afternoon swinging
a blind eye out to sea. The light
fails, day closes around me, a vast oceanic whirlpool . . .
I can still see your eyes, those monotonic palettes,
smell your whiskeyed kisses!
Still feel the eelgrass of embrace —
the ocean pounds outside the heart's door.
Dearest, the lamps are going on. I'm caught
in the smell of whales burning! Vaporous and drowsy,
I spiral down the staircase in my wrapper,
a shadow among many shadows in Nantucket Town.
Out in the yard, the chinaberry tree
turns amber. A hymn spreads through the deepening air —
the church steeple's praying for the people. Last night
I dreamed you waved farewell.
I stood upon the pier, the buoys tolling
a warning knell. Trussed in my whalebone,
I grew away from you, fluttering in the twilight,
a cutout, a fancy French silhouette.

SALEM, MASSACHUSETTS: 1692

> "*. . . there are accounts of ignorant rustics tying*
> *the thumbs and toes of a supposed witch together*
> *and throwing her into a pond, where if she floated*
> *she was a witch, and if she sank, as was most*
> *likely, she usually died from the ill usage.*
> *It is gratifying to know that Matthew Hopkins,*
> *the notorious witchfinder, met his death in this*
> *manner at the hands of some country fellows*
> *who believed him to be a wizard.*"
>
> Robert Fletcher,
> *The Witches' Pharmacopoeia*

You also believed, Matthew Hopkins,
that we had a third teat and a *witch's spot*
which, when probed with pins or needles, was insensitive
to pain. How you could disregard the terrible shrieks
from those who knew nothing of our craft,
simple churchgoing women,
as well as our own, even we do not understand.

Perhaps we would have been less vengeful
if our deaths had been by fire — the exhilarating
    sensation
(after the first scalding) of going up in smoke,
of our grease dropping like rain on our sisters
enabling them
to fly through the night, uneasy shadows on your
        bedroom wall.
 Or even being hung,
a quick snap of the neck, nothing more, then the planting
in the ground, in the crevice near Gallows Hill where
    twenty-two were hung,

and nurturing the mandrake, belladonna, nightshade —
demons from which our powers are derived.

Anything but this jelly to strain through,
the eternal shiver,
the feeling of being in a fog, of never seeing the moon!

We made you look a little strange
to those twisted rustics hungry for another victim.
The earlobes, just a little too pointed,
the hair tinged with trickles of green.
And during the trial,
remember when your nervous laugh and protestations
dissolved into unwilling cackles? So terrrifying
the children rolled on the floor foaming at the mouth!
We were responsible for it all.
We were waiting for you, Matthew Hopkins, down there
under the dull pond water. We had all the time
    in the world
to untie our thumbs and toes,
draw the pins out of our skirts, pricks up,
then wait as you floated down
instead of up,
proving not that you were our kind,
but only a torturer, the weakest sort of man.

EXHUMATION

for Elizabeth Siddall (1832–1862),
wife of Dante Gabriel Rossetti

You shut me up in a cold box and buried me
just because I died   at first I thought
I'd never forgive you that
the turning away
the last of many desertions

I rotted   slowly and without anguish
gracefully
flesh falling from my arms   fingertips turning to mush
my teeth blossoming into a huge smile
    eight years I thought about my life among the living
    the afternoons slowly escaping through rose-stained windows
    the smoke of women's hair moving among men
    the dew rising from fields in solid, shining points

And in the end, my thoughts always returned to you, Dante
to the dissatisfactions
that had hovered between us like small grey clouds

Then   gradually   you fell away
into the cold blankness of time
became otherworldly so I could no longer understand
but your poems
your gift to me on the first day of my death
they stayed with me
they were there   next to my cheek
    something I could never say of you with your brothel nights
    and your distaste for my body —
    the possessing, I mean

Then   when I was only bone and no longer a treasure
you dug me up
rude jolting from the dream!
the terrible reawakening to trees and the color of the sky!
oh   the silence I screamed as light swarmed into my marrow
as you rifled me
taking the poems tied with my hair   bound in my skin
not looking into the sockets where my eyes had swum
    believing I was gone like a lightless traveller
                        heartless   I wanted to call you
inhuman as you stood above me all human and living
a vulture   a circling black thing

It was then that I clutched myself into a cold hard ball
and prepared for the second gravesleep
this time without any of the small attachments necessary
    for a woman slighted in life
this time with a hollow in my cheek

COURTESAN WITH FAN

Auspicious night.
              The stars balance on poles
as a crescent moon, half-eaten,
rises out of the persimmon tree.

The dragon at the top of the sky
flails the universe

as if I were once more seven,
my mother binding my feet into delicate hooves.
I rocked like a boat, my feet two white moons,
two crescents of pain.

Half-woman, I languished in the sequestered bedchamber
till my body sprouted —
a swollen green shoot tender to strangers.

They handle me, paint
my shoulders with their tongues.

I breathe in the blackness of complete abandon,
as if I were diving for pearls,
              deeper, deeper,
my spiderfine silks changing to seaweed.

Always when it happens, I close my eyes.
My bones bend like watery willows.
The stars, tiny mourners, go out one by one.

AFTER THREE JAPANESE DRAWINGS

Fat Man
(Shokado)

Clearly, the man eats too much.
He holds a half-eaten plum, reaches unthinking
toward the empty bowl for another one.
His manners are bad. He embarrasses his guests
by unfastening his pants, scolds
the thin children who break into his orchard
and find nothing. He thinks of himself as wise,
but look, he ignores the hovering butterfly,
smiles not at his wife, now approaching,
but at the fruit she carries.
More fruit for him.

Girl Monkey Trainer
(Kyosai)

Her family was poor. Her feet big as brooms.
No one in the village would marry her.
One night she ran away, taking
the small amount that was to be her dowry.
She met a man on the road, a man
with two monkeys. He gave her one
for spending the night with him.
Now she lives far from the provinces, smiling
often at her good fortune. Her monkey performs well.
She buys herself silk scarves, has tea
whenever she wants it, rice cakes, wine.

Yeoman Murdering His Deformed Wife with a Sickle
(Kuniyoshi)

The marriage was arranged. There were no children.
Nights when they slept, he shrank
from her side, shrivelled like snakeskin
left out in the sun. Dreamed the old men of the town
offered him their hoary cheeks to kiss.
He complained of the nettle soup she fixed,
so she fixed other soups and still he complained.
In early spring, after a winter of rain,
they stood in the garden arguing. He reached
for the sickle meaning only to cut off her hand.
But she screamed. Travellers were passing
on the bridge not far from where they stood.
Alarmed, he swung the sickle again and again
till she was quiet under him.

DEATH DRESS

A midwife wore it.
Delivering a stillborn girl,
she wiped the death off her hands on the dress.
Wiped the death off, went to the next house
and delivered twin boys with black hair.

A witch wore it.
Stuffed mandrake and belladonna into the pockets.
At nights the dress flickered in the forest,
queen of the trees, a crazy apparition.
A black stone is her pillow.

A nun wore it.
Her skin turned transparent with fear and longing.
She stuck a crucifix through her heart.
A page in her Bible turned black.

A widow put it on.
She choked on lamentations,
shrank into a skeleton.
The dress continued to fit perfectly.

Your friend wore it.
Three times she tried to take it off.
The third time the buttons burnt her fingers.
She stuck her head in an oven.
Her head turned black.

You wore it.
You put it on your mannequin when you bathed.
You slept in it, dreamt
it was your invention.
It grew black roots into your brain.

You were not buried in it.
It is not a dress to be buried in.
You wore it, and now you give it to me.
Regal and elegant, I stand here stiffly in this black.
Unready, unwilling, I give it back.

THE TRAVELLERS

We have black teeth but we dream just the
same as the people who live in houses.
                    Janine Wiedel and
                  Martina O'Fearadhaigh,
                              Irish Tinkers

When the lake lies still as a mirror,
giving the sky back every star it has stolen,
when the moon bleaches our nightclothes
white as the shirts that flutter in store windows,
when fog erases the walls you have built,
stone by stone, to keep us out,
                              then we will come,
driving our wagons through your painted dreams,
entering your houses on tiptoe.
We've brought the tin cup
you never bought from us, a penny
for your tongue since you like the taste
of money. We've brought our daughters and sons,
the dead ones, who whisper and sing
as they go through your children's playthings.
They beg us to stay awhile, they say
they are cold and want to drink all the milk
they can hold. But we are travellers.
We know it's bad luck taking the dead on the road.
We'll leave them here, stopping again
in a year or a week or tomorrow.

You wake up sweating, feverish.
Your blankets are gone, all the windows
in your house are open.
You will never catch us.

We have taken the crooked road
to the next county, the trees hurrying
us along, pointing *this way*, *this way*,
with their crooked arms.
But the little ghosteens stay on,
hiding in closets and cupboards, whispering:
We are the rag and bone.
We are the summer walkers of the long acre.
We've come to pick the potato eyes
out of the quality folk,
to comb the gristle out of the meat
of the country men.

III

SNOWFALL

1.
Day of the first snow
I wake
to the negative music of silence,
cold blue bars of light
falling on tables, on chairs.
My arms are blue.
I'm a blue nude stumbling to the bath.
Touch water. Touch soap.
The dream comes back to me now —
desire's glass eye outside the window,
footprints tracking toward the horizon.
Smaller, smaller, black crow-tracks,
black points in the snow. Nothing.

2.
Strange journeys we made toward each other!
Us, and of course, all the others.
Slowly, as if on snowshoes, crossing
the darkening tundra of memory
while night repeated itself above our heads —
a kind of unrelenting leitmotif
in the symphony of mind.
At times you were a hallucination.
At times I was lost in a whiteout,
not only to the world,
but to myself. If only I could have verified
the truth as easily as ringing a triad
of glass bells,
their resolute notes leaving us untroubled, yet wise,
passionate, and still young!
As if the world could suddenly tilt

into a fifth season, the icescape melt,
leaving our voices
high and melodic in the rarified air.
Flowers and winter breathing in tandem!
Your body filling me with snow!

3.
Outside the window the fields
open themselves
once more to snowfall, each tree
stands erect and alone in its icing of snow.
Inside this room the heart beats
in delicate counterpoint
to the inevitable snows of the future.
Inside my body
it is snowing.

BLUE NUDE

It is not true
what they say about the body:
that it must be loved, that it cannot
sleep through its nights alone
without injury.

Look at me. Look
at the way the artist lies
about his loneliness, painting a room
where walls, floor, and ceiling
converge on a door too small

for me to leave or enter.
Leaving my face featureless as snow,
my body bruised like the pears
he buys only to paint.
They should have been eaten weeks ago.

Swollen and isolate, they sit
on a bone-white plate, their shadows
distortions of their true shape,
ellipses of blue and darker
blue the eye falls into.

Only I know
how the snow fell for days
outside his studio, how he painted
in his coat and gloves,
rising each morning

to break the ice in the washbowl
and light the stove,
the heart of the flame
blue against his chest.
The heart, he thinks, *the heart*

is blue and solitary.
It knows what it knows.
And so he paints a room
with one of everything:
one bed with one pillow,

one window overlooking
shadowed figures walking
two by two, one book whose pages
turn as days do, each page only
part of a larger story.

INSTRUCTIONS FOR THE SLEEPER

Dreamingly the spirit projects its own
reality, but this reality is nothing.
                                    Kierkegaard

Touch
those that you love
only during sleep
when the woman sleeps
in her father's hand
and the man curls into sleep
as a bone curls into flesh.
The sleeper will come
to you then, asking
nothing, carrying
bright empty packages
that belong to no one.

Within my arms he sleeps, safe
from himself, far from what hurts him.
We walk in the dark like children, hand in hand,
lay ourselves down in the thin white clothes
of exhaustion. I guard his sleep with mine,
guard sleep's secrets by not moving.

Tell
no one what you did.
In the morning hide desire's
presents till it's night
again. They lie
by the bed unopened,
as if the gift of yourself
were enough to ease

the sleeper's dawn,
restore the dream, now
receding, that continues
without you or anyone.

THE TELESCOPE

It looked like any other town, only smaller.
There was a town square with a white tower
rising above trees tall as my thumbnail.
And painted storefronts out of a fairytale
with signboards advertising the town's wares.

Ships came and went in the harbor,
each one small as a ship in a bottle, but where
they were sailing to and whether it proved
the world was round or flat didn't matter.
(I hadn't felt the urge to travel yet.)

The sun behind my back, I saw the Spectacle
Shop look back, two eyes outlined on wood
in black, I saw the butcher's blade
sharpen itself on the block, paring the heart
from its cage of bone, I saw prisms and gears

and clocks striking in unison the hours
of forgetfulness. I lay in the fields, sleeping
whenever the town slept, dreaming myself
small as a key in a lock, then smaller still.
Or sleepless, I circled the town searching

for lighted windows, but the rooms were
poorly lit and the people only shadows;
when they touched each other,
their actions gave me pain, not pleasure,
and then I'd give up looking for an hour.

Years passed and the faces grew familiar,
and after many years I recognized myself —
not as I am now but as a child
(nobody in the town ever grew older) —
playing the children's games, blindfolded,

staggering, or locked in a circle of hands
as the bigger children danced around
the others. But each time I stepped forward
to see better, the telescope I was holding
made the town seem smaller, till finally

no matter which lenses I used or
in what order, I knew there was a limit
on my sight, that years of vigilance were
unaccounted for. What could I hope for?
The child in the long skirts would

stay there past my life, accomplice to
cruelty and tenderness, the backward motion
of the children's dance reversing time's
advance. I left in the middle of the night,
not knowing where I would go,

the children's shouts following
me across the fields, fainter now,
but clear, untouchable stars burning
five-pointed holes in the dark, grieving,
leaving behind a useless telescope.

BLAME

I do not believe the ancients —
the constellations look like nothing at all.

See how their light scatters itself
across the sky, not bright

enough to guide us anywhere?
And the avenues of trees, leaking

their dark inks, are shapes I can't identify.
The night is too inconstant, a constant

injury, alchemical moonlight
changing my body from lead to silver,

silver to lead. I lie
uncovered on the bed, unmoved

by the love you left, bad dreams,
bad night ahead. All summer

you held me to your chest:
It's the heat, you said, accounting

for our sleeplessness, so that
touch became metaphor for what kept us

separate. Our lives construct
themselves out of the lie of pain.

I lied when I sent you away.
To call your name would be another lie.

DARK NIGHT ON CAPE COD

No light on a night like this, no stars,
no words that can bring you to me . . .

The stars, the sea, the sound of the sea, the night,
can't be touched
though I reach out my hands into darkness.
The jetty is anchored in rock
that stops
the ocean's violence and under the waves
a black floor
slants down and down
and that's where the drowned walk,
calling to no one, wordlessly
waiting
to be found. Imagine
their mouths: struck in attitudes
of despair, like Leonardo's
drawings of the damned,
each leaf on the Paradisal trees
in the background carefully heightened in silverpoint.
And their hearts: blue aureoles
of light expanding
like stars
in the infinite hollows of the chest
until the body is its own testament.

I lean into the wind, a struck match
flaring against the dark.

No light on a night like this, no stars,
no words that can bring you to me. . . .

SUN IN AN EMPTY ROOM

after the Edward Hopper painting

Gone the longing which held him back from sleep,
a wound of emptiness which would not heal itself,
till dawn made ragged curtains of the night's
black cloth, light entering the room
as the white smell of salt did when the tides
turned toward land, touching him as music,
or a woman's hand, could not, and he slept,
sun striking the west wall again and again,
another canvas ready to be painted.

LETTERS TO THE SEA

1. Swimming at Midnight
7. 7. 77

Moonlight chisels your face into marble skin.
Arm over arm, we swim,
carrying old virtues like half-drowned children.
You speak your desire, scattering
the moon's reflection:
bright tin foil floating on water.
I touch your chest. Phosphor
flares inside you like a match.

We turn on touch, and touching,
turn into something else.
Stars chant incantations above our heads.
There's my dark twin, Gemini,
slicing the sky into lucky number sevens.
You're Pisces — half-man,
half-fish, you swim outside time's net
and take me along for the ride.

We fall asleep at dawn, two
breaths blending into one.
Now birds begin the cries that people waking
call bird song.

2. The Hill

White hill caught in the sun. Green water.
I see you as you are: a man
wrapped in the white skin of winter
trying to take it off.
We move through impossible hours of desire.
In one month, two, you'll be the ghost
my hand passes through in sleep,
the vague shadow at breakfast
pulling me back to a place I woke from.
But now you touch me as a widow's grief
touches a mirror: unclouded silver
changing to ocean without center or shore.

3. The Fortune

Eye to unseeing eye, she
sits with her back to me,
telling the beads on her rosary,
stirring her black tea.

Why have you come?
There's nobody here.
I live with no one.

— You lost a lover to the sea.
You lost a son.
The women in black shawls told me.

I lost no one.
What do you want from me?

—A prophecy. That's why I've come.

I've lied to others. I'll lie to you.
A siren sings more sweetly than I do.

—Old woman, tell me.

Ring finger cut off at the knuckle,
she points at me:

Yours is a young song, full of folly.
No one will mourn you. No one mourns me.

4. Stones

Nights without sleep!
The terrible cries of the birds at dawn!
Each day I carry stones to the sea, first
to the shallows, then to the deep end of the bay.
Each night he enters me,
warming the stone between my legs with his.

I fill my plate with a broth of stones,
hold stones in my hands when I sleep.
And still I'm not safe.
I must go away.
The walls of this house will crush me.

A stone boat sails under the waves.
Then let the sea take me.

5. Wake

Ash in the air. Ash in everyone's mouth.
You wake to a room without doors or windows.
You should have known.
Last night the oil lamp hissed, wick
twisting into a death you didn't recognize.
And now the wet wood of the body will not rise.
Listen. They call you, black-shawled women,
crows glittering in their palaces of straw.
Forget them. Go to the dead place
the dead know losing your past
as snow loses itself on water. Go now
or the trees will touch their fingertips
to yours. I am your soul.
I am who you turn to when the world stops.

6. Departing the Place Where You Stand

Pared-down, white-skinned, and alone,
a marble sea cliff arches against the dawn.
Now let the sun climb over the ocean's hill,
stopping to rest on a higher hill in the air.
Spasms of light dress me in longing.
I'm flower sprouting from stone,
a long, clean shadow licked by the sea's
tongue. What I see, I see
for the first time: clouds forming themselves
into shapes of loss, horizon straining to catch them.

I rise, white-winged, small-hearted, and
devout. My sorrow is buried in the country of doubt.
I was pallbearer. I wrote its epitaph.
I dug the grave. I planted flowers in its mouth.

Here, take this, though you are far away.
My motion shapes the world and shapes myself.

About the Author

Elizabeth Spires was graduated from Vassar
College in 1974 and received her M.A. from the
Johns Hopkins University. She won the W.K.
Rose Fellowship in the Creative Arts from
Vassar College in 1976 and an Individual Artist's
Grant from the Ohio Arts Council in 1978. She
has worked as a freelance writer and editor for a
publishing company in Columbus, Ohio, and has
taught at Washington College in Chestertown,
Maryland. Her poetry has been published in
*The Yale Review, The New Yorker, Partisan Review,
Poetry, Paris Review,* and *Antaeus,* and in a
number of other journals.

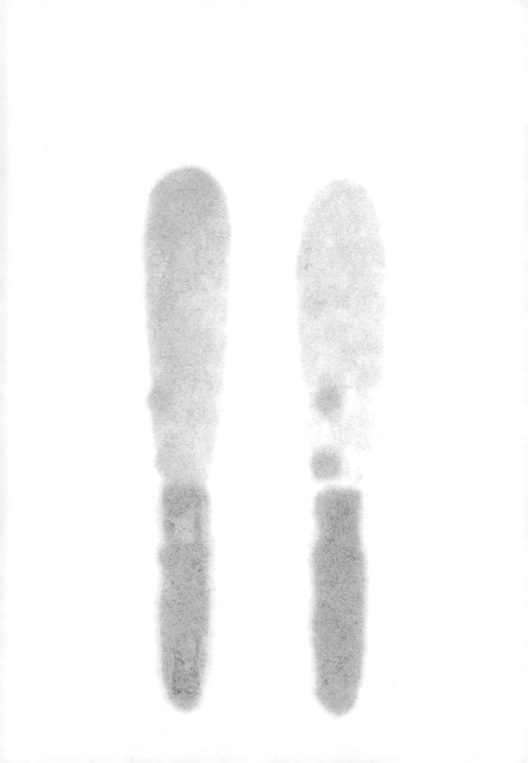

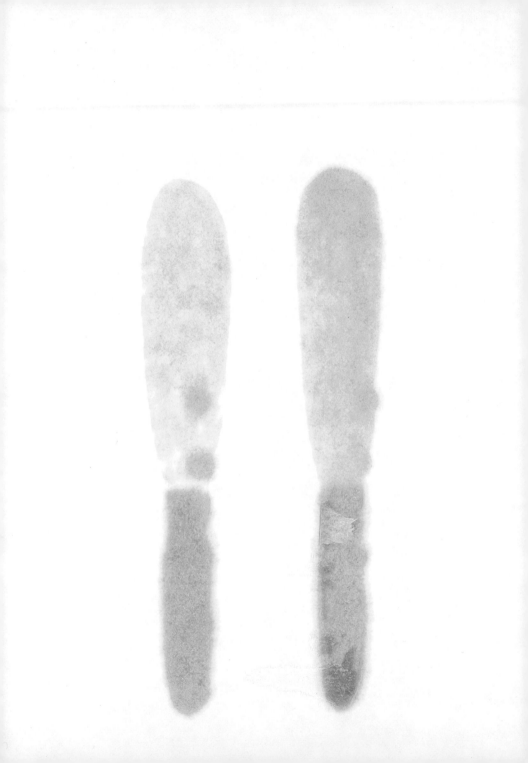